WISDOM

It Is Not For Sale

Dr. Laura Thompson

TM
Laura Thompson Ministries

ISBN-13: 978-0615648132

ISBN-10: 0615648134

Printed in the U.S.A.

First Edition

WISDOM
It Is Not For Sale

Dr. Laura Thompson

Laura Thompson Ministries ™

Acknowledgements

I am grateful to my husband, Marvin, for his faithfulness. I thank my children for always inspiring me. I would like to personally thank Dr. Amanda Goodson for the "PUSH" and her continuing support. To the Open Door Church family, my sons and daughters in ministry, for their faithfulness; Thanks.

TABLE OF CONTENTS

FORWARD

There are multiplicities of things in life that can be obtained monetarily, but wisdom is not one of them (Proverbs 23:23). It's only through our relationship with the Father, that godly wisdom is obtained. Life is full of perplexities and an unwise individual could very easily become hopeless. Only those who are wise will see through the forest and not be distracted or stifled by the trees.

Today we are faced with so many distractions and often times are unsure as to how, or if, we can move beyond them. *Wisdom: It Is not For Sale* will provide the answers. In the pages that follow, you will find keys that will unlock doors of generational ignorance. This book is overflowing with Kingdom Keys that will bless you and help catapult you into your next dimension in God.

Apostle Laura M. Thompson is a woman of wisdom. It's by wisdom that she has guided many men and women into their destiny. Now, the Lord has released her to impart globally through the pages of this book. Her life is devoted to Kingdom service, having the end-time mandate to help equip and activate God's end-time army. She has provided the greatest strategy ever–pursue God like never before!!!

This book is powerful, practical, and full of wise principles. It's an excellent tool for personal, group, or cooperate study. Apostle Laura Thompson will empower you to seize every opportunity that the Father presents.

Read and Reap!

Apostle Sylvia Moore

INTRODUCTION

I was praying and wondering at the same time about these critical concerns: Why we have lost precious time and anointing from God, and are looking for answers that would draw us back to God. Why has the Body of Christ been under attack? Churches and leaders are in disarray. What is missing? The hunger for God is at an all-time low. We are saying with our mouths that we need Him; yet we are just existing. This morning at 3:30 am, God spoke and said, "It's not for sale– WISDOM."

We will need to get back to the basic things, in order to regain the ground that has been lost. We must begin seeking God with our whole bodies, minds, and strength. It is imperative that we get closer to God because we are closer to the last days than we believe. Let us look again at what it will take for us to cause wisdom to be restored, refocused, and replenished in the Church, in leaders, and in the people of God.

I have prayed that when you have finished this book, we will seek and refurbish wisdom and all of her principles back in position in the Kingdom of God.

Dr. T

1. The Three Concepts of Wisdom

Wisdom is the ability to make wise decisions, and to have knowledge of what is true or right, coupled with discernment or insight.

"And you shall do what is right and good in the sight of the LORD, *that it may be well with you." (Deut. 6:18a)*

Often times we may know what is right, but we don't do it, nor do we make the right choice. Even when it comes down to just choosing the right friend or being with the wrong crowd when you know it's not the best thing to do. You have to develop insight to look ahead to see where this is going to take you and decide whether or not where it will take you will be beneficial in life. Throughout the book of Proverbs we are instructed on how to be wise.

"The fear of the Lord is the beginning of knowledge." (Proverbs 1:7a)

I believe there are three concepts of wisdom you must obtain to become wise. Knowledge, Instructions, Understanding. Let's call them the KIU's of wisdom.

In the book of Proverbs, these three words are used consistently to bring clarity to whatever issues we are facing. Let's look at Knowledge. Knowledge is the acquaintance with facts, truths, or principles as from study or investigation.

"Wise people store up knowledge, But the mouth of the foolish is near destruction." *(Proverbs 10:14)*

"Now two women who were harlots came to the king, and stood before him. And one woman said, "O my lord, this woman and I dwell in the same house; and I gave birth while she was in the house. Then it happened, the third day after I had given birth, that this woman also gave birth. And we were together; no one was with us in the house, except the two of us in the house. And this woman's son died in the night, because she lay on him. So she arose in the middle of the night and took my son from my side, while your maidservant slept, and laid him in her bosom, and laid her dead child in my bosom. And when I rose in the morning to nurse my son, there he was, dead. But when I had examined him in the morning, indeed, he was not my son whom I had borne." Then the other woman said, "No! But the living one is my son, and the dead one is your son." And the first woman said, "No! But the dead one is your son, and the living one is my son." Thus they spoke before the king. And the king said, "The one says, 'This is my son, who lives, and your son is the dead one'; and the other says, 'No! But your son is the dead one, and my son is the living one.'" Then the king said, "Bring me a sword." So they brought a sword before the king. And the king said, "Divide the living child in two, and give half to one, and half to the other." Then the woman whose son was living spoke to the king, for she yearned with compassion for her son; and she said, "O my lord, give her the living child, and by no means kill him!" But the other said, "Let him be neither mine nor yours, but divide him." So the king answered and said, "Give the first

woman the living child, and by no means kill him; she is his mother." (1 Kings 3:16-27)

King Solomon was hearing the case of the two mothers, and as king he served as a judge, and he sought out Knowledge of the truth. By listening and observing, he made the decision to cut the baby in two. The real mother pleaded for him to spare the child. People will lie to make themselves look good or accuse you of doing or being wrong. In other words, the two mothers would have continued to go back and forth until he said divide the child. No real mother would want anything to happen to any child. It is important to investigate (look into) the causes of problems before we take one side or the other. You must listen and allow the Holy Spirit that is in you to discern every act, thought, or deed.

Let's look at the second KIU.

"Take firm hold of instruction, do not let go; Keep her, for she is your life." (Proverbs 4:13)

"Now an old prophet dwelt in Bethel, and his sons came and told him all the works that the man of God had done that day in Bethel; they also told their father the words which he had spoken to the king. And their father said to them, "Which way did he go?" For his sons had seen which way the man of God went who came from Judah. Then he said to his sons, "Saddle the donkey for me." So they saddled the donkey for him; and he rode on it, and went after the man of God, and found him sitting under an oak. Then he said to him, "Are you the man of God who came from Judah?" And he said, "I am." Then he said to him, "Come home with me and eat bread." And he said, "I cannot return with you nor go in with you; neither can I eat bread nor drink water with you in this place. For I have been told by the word of the LORD, 'You shall not eat bread nor drink water there, nor return by going the way you came.'" He said to him, "I too am a

prophet as you are, and an angel spoke to me by the word of the LORD, saying, 'Bring him back with you to your house, that he may eat bread and drink water.'" (He was lying to him.) So he went back with him, and ate bread in his house, and drank water. Now it happened, as they sat at the table, that the word of the LORD came to the prophet who had brought him back; and he cried out to the man of God who came from Judah, saying, "Thus says the LORD: 'Because you have disobeyed the word of the LORD, and have not kept the commandment which the LORD your God commanded you, but you came back, ate bread, and drank water in the place of which the LORD said to you, "Eat no bread and drink no water," your corpse shall not come to the tomb of your fathers.'" So it was, after he had eaten bread and after he had drunk, that he saddled the donkey for him, the prophet whom he had brought back. When he was gone, a lion met him on the road and killed him. And his corpse was thrown on the road, and the donkey stood by it. The lion also stood by the corpse. And there, men passed by and saw the corpse thrown on the road, and the lion standing by the corpse. Then they went and told it in the city where the old prophet dwelt. Now when the prophet who had brought him back from the way heard it, he said, "It is the man of God who was disobedient to the word of the LORD. Therefore the LORD has delivered him to the lion, which has torn him and killed him, according to the word of the LORD which He spoke to him." And he spoke to his sons, saying, "Saddle the donkey for me." So they saddled it. Then he went and found his corpse thrown on the road, and the donkey and the lion standing by the corpse. The lion had not eaten the corpse nor torn the donkey. And the prophet took up the corpse of the man of God, laid it on the donkey, and brought it back. So the old prophet came to the city to mourn, and to bury him. Then he laid the corpse in his own tomb; and they mourned over him, saying, "Alas, my brother!" So it was, after he had buried him, that he spoke to his sons, saying, "When I am dead, then bury me in the tomb where the man of God is buried; lay my bones beside his bones." (1 Kings 13:11-31)

When you receive instructions, follow them completely and do not let anyone pull you from them. We must take the Word of the Lord seriously, so that we may become better. This story tells us of a young prophet who had received direct instructions from God. His instructions were very specific. He let an old prophet persuade him to come to his house, eat, and dine with him. The old prophet lied to him, resulting in the young prophet's death; which could have been avoided.

When we follow God's instructions, it will lead to life and not death. Obedience is better than sacrifice, and God will never deceive you. Can you remember having to take tests in school? Each section had its own instructions. If you wanted to pass the test, you were required to read each section and follow the directions.

"This Book of the Law shall not depart from your mouth, but you shall meditate in it day and night, that you may observe to do according to all that is written in it. For then you will make your way prosperous, and then you will have good success." (Joshua 1:8)

Our third KIU is Understanding. Good understanding wins favor.

"A righteous man hates lying." (Proverbs 13:5a)

Understanding causes us to recognize who, what, when, where, how, and why.

"They are all plain to him who understands, and right to those who find knowledge. Receive my instruction, and not silver, and knowledge rather than choice gold; For wisdom is

better than rubies, and all the things one may desire cannot be compared with her." (Proverb 8: 9-11)

"Then you will understand righteousness and justice, equity and every good path." (Proverb 2:9)

"All the women who were gifted artisans spun yarn with their hands, and brought what they had spun, of blue, purple, and scarlet, and fine linen. And all the women whose hearts stirred with wisdom spun yarn of goats' hair. The rulers brought onyx stones, and the stones to be set in the ephod and in the breastplate, and spices and oil for the light, for the anointing oil, and for the sweet incense. The children of Israel brought a freewill offering to the LORD, all the men and women whose hearts were willing to bring material for all kinds of work which the LORD, by the hand of Moses, had commanded to be done. And Moses said to the children of Israel, "See, the LORD has called by name Bezalel the son of Uri, the son of Hur, of the tribe of Judah; and He has filled him with the Spirit of God, in wisdom and understanding, in knowledge and all manner of workmanship, to design artistic works, to work in gold and silver and bronze, in cutting jewels for setting, in carving wood, and to work in all manner of artistic workmanship. "And He has put in his heart the ability to teach, in him and Aholiab the son of Ahisamach, of the tribe of Dan. He has filled them with skill to do all manner of work of the engraver and the designer and the tapestry maker, in blue, purple, and scarlet thread, and fine linen, and of the weaver—those who do every work and those who design artistic works." (Ex.35:25-35)

When wisdom is stirred up in the hearts of men and women nothing is impossible for them to accomplish. God called Bezalel by name, and filled him with the Spirit of God in wisdom in understanding, and in knowledge, and in all manner of workmanship. Wisdom was imputed in him that he may teach others skills in order to build the Kingdom.

God has work for everyone to do. We must do things right to have a correct and righteous response. We must move past just giving God anything while still expecting His blessings. We must diligently seek knowledge as to how things must be built. Even in establishing a relationship with God, be honest and stop being in a hurry to get things done. Build line upon line, and precept on precept, knowing that except God build it, our labor is in vain.

I learned this little proverb in the third grade, "If a task is once begun, never leave it until it's done. Be a laborer, great or small; do it well, or not at all." I have learned that not everyone moves at the same pace. Do not quit; allow each day to bring you closer to God and what He wants you to be. God will develop the ministry gift/gifts in you. The KUI's give you strength, power, and direction to move forward in every path in which God will lead you.

"And Bezalel and Aholiab, and every gifted artisan in whom the LORD has put wisdom and understanding, to know how to do all manner of work for the service of the sanctuary, shall do according to all that the LORD has commanded." Then Moses called Bezalel and Aholiab, and every gifted artisan in whose heart the LORD had put wisdom, everyone whose heart was stirred, to come and do the work. And they received from Moses all the offering which the children of Israel had brought for the work of the service of making the sanctuary. So they continued bringing to him freewill offerings every morning. Then all the craftsmen who were doing all the work of the sanctuary came, each from the work he was doing." (Exodus 36:1-4)

Just as God gave them wisdom, He will do the same for you. I pray that you will ask God to stir up His Spirit within you, take you off delay, and again place you in line with destiny. This time you will make good and wise decisions.

2. Releasing the Compass

"The LORD possessed me at the beginning of His way, before His works of old. I have been established from everlasting, from the beginning, before there was ever an earth. When there were no depths I was brought forth, when there were no fountains abounding with water. Before the mountains were settled, before the hills, I was brought forth; While as yet He had not made the earth or the fields, Or the primal dust of the world. When He prepared the heavens, I was there, when He drew a circle on the face of the deep, When He established the clouds above, when He strengthened the fountains of the deep, When He assigned to the sea its limit, so that the waters would not transgress His command, when He marked out the foundations of the earth, Then I was beside Him as a master craftsman; and I was daily His delight, rejoicing always before Him, Rejoicing in His inhabited world, and my delight was with the sons of men. "Now therefore, listen to me, my children, for blessed are those who keep my ways. Hear instruction and be wise, and do not disdain it. Blessed is the man who listens to me, watching daily at my gates, waiting at the posts of my doors. For whoever finds me finds life, and obtains favor from the LORD; But he who sins against me wrongs his own soul; all those who hate me love death."
(Proverbs 8:22-36)

Wisdom has been here from the beginning. The word wisdom can be used interchangeably with Jesus. The scripture says that the Lord possessed us in the beginning; before the earth was ever created. The Godhead took time to think and plan creation and to set things in the earth that would be necessary for us.

"The earth is the LORD's, and all its fullness, the world and those who dwell therein." (Ps.24:1)

We may learn to draw out from it the things for survival. Have you ever considered why God made you from the ground and placed everything you need within you? As I studied this scripture, the Lord began to speak me.

"When He prepared the heavens, I was there." (Proverbs 8:27b)

He set a compass upon the face of the deep. Before God created you, He placed a navigation system inside of you so that you would always have a sense of direction and be able to get from point A to point B. In Genesis 15:7, God told Abraham to leave the land of Ur of the Chaldees. A sense of direction had to be in him in order for him to take up everything and leave, not knowing the physical direction in which God was taking him. The compass is not only a means of direction for travel, it is also a line of thought.

"Now Jabez was more honorable than his brothers, and his mother called his name Jabez, saying, "Because I bore him in pain." And Jabez called on the God of Israel saying, "Oh, that You would bless me indeed, and enlarge my territory, that Your hand would be with me, and that You would keep me from evil, that I may not cause pain!" So God granted him what he requested." (1 Chronicles 4:9-10)

Jabez was an honorable man who made his request known unto God. His request was for God to bless him, indeed; to enlarge his coast; for God's hand be upon him to keep him from evil so it may not grieve him. In everything He asked of God, it was granted.

"Be anxious for nothing, but in everything by prayer and supplication, with thanksgiving, let your requests be made known to God." (Philippians 4:6)

Jabez made his request known unto God; asking for His guidance to be successful, to be able to maintain his success, and to not become greedy. When we do this, God will lead and guide us into all truth.

"Lead me in Your truth and teach me, for You are the God of my salvation; on You I wait all the day." (Psalms 25:5)

The compass has another function, or in other words, it has another Name. The Holy Ghost within you, will guide and teach you to go beyond your physical limitations and will stretch you into purpose. The Holy Ghost will ignite ministry gifts and unlock treasures. The bible teaches us that the weapons of our warfare are not carnal but mighty through God to the pulling down of strongholds (see 2 Corinthians 10:4). The Holy Ghost will teach you how to become a weapon, and with accuracy, how to defeat the enemy in his own territory. As you grow, you will lead people to Jesus Christ by showing them His ways, causing them to become fishers of men.

In the earth, boundaries have been established. The rivers only run over their banks when God allows them to do so. However, He takes the limits off you. No one can tell you how deep you can go in Him. All that is required is that you allow Jesus to lead you to your expected end.

3. The Principle Thing

First, let me start by saying that I am a firm believer in people working hard to maintain healthy living, relationships, work history, and ethics. In other words, I am a firm believer in working the basic bible principles. The word principle means an accepted or professed rule of action or conduct. Basic bible principles allow individuals to make good, sound, and wise decisions. People making wise decisions are ones who understand that it is more important to be safe than sorry.

Wisdom is the ability to make right decisions and to choose the correct solution for any situation. It knows how to think, speak, and act to please God and be at peace with man. It is the basis for victorious living. Without wisdom, people make choices that bring them pain, poverty, trouble, and even death. With wisdom, people make choices that bring them health, peace, prosperity, and life.

What are basic bible principles? I'm so glad you asked!

1. Do unto others, as you would have them do unto you.
2. Love thy neighbor as thy self.
3. Seek ye first the Kingdom of God and His righteousness, and all these things shall be added unto you.

I call these basic bible principles; simple instructions that Christians should follow daily.

"Wisdom is the principal thing; Therefore get wisdom. And in all your getting, get understanding." (Proverbs 4:7)

One simple thing about wisdom is what the elder saints called a 'bought lesson.' Once you learn from a situation, you apply the wisdom that you have gained to your next circumstance.

"Help, LORD, for the godly man ceases! For the faithful disappear from among the sons of men. They speak idly everyone with his neighbor; With flattering lips and a double heart they speak." (Psalms 12:1-2)

This scripture tells us that people have stopped being men and women of integrity. We seek to take care of ourselves first, leaving everyone else to fit wherever they can. I remember when older people would pray for their neighbors and their neighbor's children. This was a time when people helped you raise your children; but now you cannot trust your children with everybody. Perversion is on the rampage, and the place where they were once safe no longer exists. The church and schools have become polluted. Morals have been removed, and everybody is doing what they think is right in their own eyes (see Judges 21:25). We must return to bible principles. The Word of God provides principles that need to be worked in our lives.

"Now to Him who is able to do exceedingly abundantly above all that we ask or think, according to the power that works in us." (Ephesians 3:20)

This scripture, which is often quoted, is a principle. Let's examine it:

Now unto Him (when you see yourself in Christ, this statement should speak clearly to you, about you): The first step is that your expectation must be turned up. Work this principle. The process begins the moment you conceive an idea or a thought. Where you take it, or how deep you take it, is up to you.

God lets us know that greatness is within us. When does the release start? The moment God releases the Word concerning you; your dialogue, remembering the spoken Word over your life, immediately starts applying. May I pause and ask: we are expecting it, right?

The next step is you being able to work on you, now. Working on your means being able to physically, mentally, and spiritually bombard heaven for the strength to release your treasure in the earth, and to come forth and manifest. How much will be released will be according to the power that lies within you. "If a task is once begun, never leave until it's done. Be a laborer, great or small. Do it well, or not at all."

I put my little quotation there because it's going to take a lot of work to pull off the demonstration of the manifestation of the principle of the greatness of God being released in you. God is causing your mouth, heart, and spirit to become ONE. Your spirit will receive it, your heart becomes overwhelmed with it, and then your mouth will speak it.

Expect the greatness to be unlocked in you. Then restoration can come to the house of God, so we that live by the gospel can demonstrate godly principles again.

4. The Cries of Wisdom

Have you ever listened and heard someone crying? It can be quite disturbing. The sound of agony and grief causes one's heart to be in much pain. When I think of wisdom crying, I think of a person crying uncontrollably and unable to stop, seeing the state of man's condition and how help is continually refused.

"Wisdom cries aloud in the street, she raises her voice in the markets; She cries at the head of the noisy intersections [in the chief gathering places]; at the entrance of the city gates she speaks: How long, O simple ones [open to evil], will you love being simple? And the scoffers delight in scoffing and [self-confident] fools hate knowledge? If you will turn (repent) and give heed to my reproof, behold, I [Wisdom] will pour out my spirit upon you, I will make my words known to you. Because I have called and you have refused [to answer], have stretched out my hand and no man has heeded it, And you treated as nothing all my counsel and would accept none of my reproof, I also will laugh at your calamity; I will mock when the thing comes that shall cause you terror and panic."
(Proverbs 1: 20- 26 AMP)

"Wisdom cries aloud in the street, she raises her voice in the markets." (Proverbs 1:20 AMP)

Wisdom is shouting for us to pay attention and take a close look at what's happening. There are traps set for you to fall into. Wake up. Wisdom is travailing for her children; remember what I have taught you.

"MY SON, if you will receive my words and treasure up my commandments within you, Making your ear attentive to skillful and godly Wisdom and inclining and directing your heart and mind to understanding [applying all your powers to the quest for it]; Yes, if you cry out for insight and raise your voice for understanding." (Proverbs 2:1-3 AMP)

We must not continue to fall prey to injustices, premature deaths, and mishaps. We must cry aloud and spare not.

"CRY ALOUD, spare not. Lift up your voice like a trumpet and declare to My people their transgression and to the house of Jacob their sins." (Isaiah 58:1)

The gospel of Jesus Christ, the following of His teaching, and adhering to His ways provides the answer to everything that is happening in our lives. There is a sound being released in the earth. The plants and animals are paying attention; but we are not. There are changes occurring in the planets and the sun. Things are aligning themselves in preparation for the shift in the atmosphere. We continue to ignore our surroundings, while everything is changing. God has released the sound for the church to come together. We must put aside our personal agendas, differences, and the things that separate us, and come together; touching and agreeing and placing God in our midst.

"For where two or three are gathered together in My name, I am there in the midst of them." (Matthew 18:20)

30

Wisdom is crying because we have forgotten our weapons of warfare.

"If My people, who are called by My name, shall humble themselves, pray, seek, crave, and require of necessity My face and turn from their wicked ways, then will I hear from heaven, forgive their sin, and heal their land." (2 Chronicles 7:14)

We have tools, gifts, and callings to use, and we must apply them. We are not defeated; we are the righteousness of God through Christ Jesus.

We must speak to the mountains and not remain silent anymore.

"Truly I tell you, whoever says to this mountain, Be lifted up and thrown into the sea! and does not doubt at all in his heart but believes that what he says will take place, it will be done for him For this reason I am telling you, whatever you ask for in prayer, believe (trust and be confident) that it is granted to you, and you will [get it]." (Mark 11:23-24 AMP)

Speak to the mountains–they can and will be removed. Have faith and trust in the Word of God that lies in you. Move past the thinking that no one is hearing you. God hears you; He needs just one person to take a stand. I know you are asking, "Just one?" Yes; one can chase a thousand, and two can chase ten thousand. Notice how God multiplies from just one person speaking out.

"And you shall chase your enemies, and they shall fall before you by the sword. Five of you shall chase a hundred, and a hundred of you shall put ten thousand to flight; your enemies shall fall before you by the sword." (Leviticus 26:7-8)

Elijah thought he was the only one left, but God spoke and revealed that He had seven thousand who had not bowed to Baal.

"And there he went into a cave, and spent the night in that place; and behold, the word of the LORD came to him, and He said to him, "What are you doing here, Elijah?" So he said, "I have been very zealous for the LORD God of hosts; for the children of Israel have forsaken Your covenant, torn down Your altars, and killed Your prophets. Then He said, "Go out, and stand on the mountain before the LORD." And behold, the LORD passed by, and a great and strong wind tore into the mountains and broke the rocks in pieces before the LORD, but the LORD was not in the wind; and after the wind an earthquake, but the LORD was not in the earthquake; and after the earthquake a fire, but the LORD was not in the fire; and after the fire a still small voice. So it was, when Elijah heard it, that he wrapped his face in his mantle and went out and stood in the entrance of the cave. Suddenly a voice came to him, and said, "What are you doing here, Elijah?" And he said, "I have been very zealous for the LORD God of hosts; because the children of Israel have forsaken Your covenant, torn down Your altars, and killed Your prophets with the sword. I alone am left; and they seek to take my life." Then the LORD said to him: "Go, return on your way to the Wilderness of Damascus; and when you arrive, anoint Hazael as king over Syria. Also you shall anoint Jehu the son of Nimshi as king over Israel. And Elisha the son of Shaphat of Abel Meholah you shall anoint as prophet in your place. It shall be that whoever escapes the sword of Hazael, Jehu will kill; and whoever escapes the sword of Jehu, Elisha will kill. Yet I have reserved seven thousand in Israel, all whose knees have not bowed to Baal, and every mouth that has not kissed him." (1 Kings 19:9-18)

The Kingdom of God needs to increase by leaps and bounds. We need growth to cause more souls to be added to the Kingdom of God.

"You are the salt of the earth; but if the salt loses its flavor, how shall it be seasoned? It is then good for nothing but to be thrown out and trampled underfoot by men." (Matthew 5:13)

We are the salt in the earth. Salt affects everything it touches; whether too little or too much, it can and will enhance the flavor. However, if the salt loses its flavor, its value decreases. You need to reenergize yourself; be restored to the original.

"Repent therefore and be converted, that your sins may be blotted out, so that times of refreshing may come from the presence of the Lord." (Acts 3:19)

The Word says repent, so that when the time of refreshing comes, you can be showered with the Spirit of God. The wisdom of God will be rekindled in your life.

"Does not wisdom cry out, and understanding lift up her voice? She takes her stand on the top of the high hill, beside the way, where the paths meet. She cries out by the gates, at the entry of the city, At the entrance of the doors: "To you, O men, I call, and my voice is to the sons of men. O you simple ones, understand prudence, and you fools, be of an understanding heart. Listen, for I will speak of excellent things, and from the opening of my lips will come right things; For my mouth will speak truth; wickedness is an abomination to my lips. All the words of my mouth are with righteousness; nothing crooked or perverse is in them. They are all plain to him who understands, and right to those who find knowledge. Receive my instruction, and not silver, and knowledge rather than choice gold." (Proverbs 8:1-10)

Wisdom stands in the paths, in high places, and in the gates of every entry way to get our attention so that we will listen and inquire of her. She shall speak truth; wisdom is calling for the return of her children. This is where you can participate.

Wisdom is asking for your help in guiding the people back to God. It is our responsibility to share what God is saying to the church. It is the church's responsibility to accept what God wants in this hour. Wisdom does not force anyone to accept what is being said. It sets the challenge there to allow wisdom to be personified in our lives.

"Wisdom calls aloud outside; She raises her voice in the open squares. She cries out in the chief concourses, at the openings of the gates in the city, She speaks her words: "How long, you simple ones, will you love simplicity? For scorners delight in their scorning, and fools hate knowledge. Turn at my rebuke; surely I will pour out my spirit on you; I will make my words known to you. Because I have called and you refused, I have stretched out my hand and no one regarded." (Proverbs 1:20-24)

I implore you; consider the current conditions of this country and the world and know that we need to pay closer attention. Let me remind you again that the Spirit of God resides in us. We should not be the last ones to know what's happening. God made us a little lower than the angels. He is mindful of us. He put us in charge and gave us dominion over His handiworks. Let us not forget His excellence, His power, His authority, His mercy, His anointing, His Name, and the fact that the Most Holy One is still in charge and will have the final SAY.

"O LORD, our Lord, How excellent is Your name in all the earth, Who have set Your glory above the heavens!" (Psalm 8:1)

5. The Power of the Tongue

The tongue is the smallest member of the body, yet it is the most powerful and the deadliest.

"Indeed, we put bits in horses' mouths that they may obey us, and we turn their whole body. Look also at ships: although they are so large and are driven by fierce winds, they are turned by a very small rudder wherever the pilot desires. Even so the tongue is a little member and boasts great things. See how great a forest a little fire kindles! And the tongue is a fire, a world of iniquity. The tongue is so set among our members that it defiles the whole body, and sets on fire the course of nature; and it is set on fire by hell. For every kind of beast and bird, of reptile and creature of the sea, is tamed and has been tamed by mankind. But no man can tame the tongue. It is an unruly evil, full of deadly poison. With it we bless our God and Father, and with it we curse men, who have been made in the similitude of God. Out of the same mouth proceed blessing and cursing. My brethren, these things ought not to be so. Does a spring send forth fresh water and bitter from the same opening? Can a fig tree, my brethren, bear olives, or a grapevine bear figs? Thus no spring yields both salt water and fresh. Who is wise and understanding among you? Let him show by good conduct

that his works are done in the meekness of wisdom." (James 3:3-13)

This scripture describes how we try to tame everything else, but not ourselves. It states how we put bits in a horse's mouth to turn its whole body. For many years we have allowed our mouths to overrule us. We have used it to put people in their places, or so we say. Many times we speak out of hurt, vexation, rejection, or just wanting to get back at someone who has insulted us.

In order to change where we desire to go, we must watch what we say. If a man cannot bridle his tongue, then his religion is in vain. Many years back I learned a valuable lesson. A person said something I did not like about my mother, and of course, I thought I had to defend my mother's honor. My mother was really saved, mind you; and so, naturally I got into trouble. My mother asked me this question, " Is that me?" My reply was, "No, mama." She asked, "Then why would you allow a lie to move you from what you know?" Then the light came on, and it has been on ever since. Do not use your tongue to curse yourself. Since that time, I have tried to improve and watch what I say.

"A man's stomach shall be satisfied from the fruit of his mouth; From the produce of his lips he shall be filled. Death and life are in the power of the tongue, And those who love it will eat its fruit." (Proverbs 18:20-21)

With the words that proceed from my mouth, I will be satisfied; and with the increase of my lips, I shall be filled. Life and death is in the power of your tongue. Allow me to pause and give you a life lesson. Stop waiting on someone else to speak into your life; take the Word of God and say what God says about you. I believe people can speak into your life. It is what you release that activates the procedure that causes the manifestation in your life. What I have learned is that we want

36

someone else to speak over us when the Word says that the power is in our mouths and the Word is near us.

"But what does it say? "The word is near you, in your mouth and in your heart" (that is, the word of faith which we preach)." (Romans 10:8)

What you seek and the things you have asked God for are in your heart. Take back your authority. You have allowed the enemy to cause you to stop speaking. There are things God wants you to speak over your life in order to build you into the spiritual house He (God) wants you to become.

"Then Jesus answered and said to them, "Most assuredly, I say to you, the Son can do nothing of Himself, but what He sees the Father do; for whatever He does, the Son also does in like manner. For the Father loves the Son, and shows Him all things that He Himself does; and He will show Him greater works than these, that you may marvel." (John 5:19-20)

Jesus says I can do what I have seen my Father do, and speak what my Father says. So come; read the Word of God and speak over yourself. Delight yourself in the Lord, and He will give you the desires of your heart.

"Delight yourself also in the LORD, and He shall give you the desires of your heart." (Psalms 37:4)

There is a song that we use to sing, "Jesus is on the mainline. Tell Him what you want." Go ahead and speak prophetically over yourself. Sometimes we are so quick to say what somebody else has said, but what are you saying about yourself? Stop trying to imitate someone else and discover you.

God has plans for your life. Dialogue with Him and see where He wants to take you. Your tongue possesses creative power. It speaks the things of God; it will enlarge your coast; and it will bring you into the now. Declare that your tongue will not now, nor ever again, be unruly because you are the righteousness of God through Christ Jesus. So, go on and declare your day and walk in the commands and blessings of God.

"The LORD will command the blessing on you in your storehouses and in all to which you set your hand, and He will bless you in the land which the LORD your God is giving you." (Deuteronomy 28:8)

Take back the power of your tongue. Jesus spoke, and it happened. The Word is nigh (near) thee; that is the Word of faith, which we preach in Romans 10:8. Prophesy to yourself. Speak life and encourage yourself. Where you might be right now might try to close in on you. Break out of the box; you are no longer bound, but free. You have desired God to move inside of you. Step on out, and just do it.

There is nothing too hard for God to do in you. Take the Jesus challenge. It's up to God to perform it.

6. Wisdom Produces Virtue

"For this very reason, adding your diligence [to the divine promises], employ every effort in exercising your faith to develop virtue (excellence, resolution, Christian energy), and in [exercising] virtue [develop] knowledge (intelligence)." (2 Peter 1:5 AMP)

"You, therefore, must be perfect [growing into complete maturity of godliness in mind and character, having reached the proper height of virtue and integrity], as your heavenly Father is perfect." (Matthew 5:48 AMP)

"FURTHERMORE, BRETHREN, we beg and admonish you in [virtue of our union with] the Lord Jesus, that [you follow the instructions which] you learned from us about how you ought to walk so as to please and gratify God, as indeed you are doing, [and] that you do so even more and more abundantly [attaining yet greater perfection in living this life]." (1 Thessalonians 4:1 AMP)

As we endeavor to become mature saints, we must put into practice the things we have learned. Growing up means putting away childish things. Every part of our lives becomes an example for somebody to follow. Keeping that which is holy becomes priority. The scripture says we must come to a proper height. What does that mean? Simply stated, with every level of responsibility, we must take care of the ministry that has been assigned to us and make sure that we assist in making people better than us.

Everything must be pleasing to God. I believe we desire to please our leaders, and that is good. God speaks to our leaders to push us farther than where we are. However, the voice coming from your leader and the voice of God should be one and the same. We must make sure that we are submitted vessels. The Spirit of Excellence is a must in the believer's life. We must remove multiple personalities from our midst and demonstrate the power of God. The scripture says, if there is any virtue pushing you to perfection, and any Christian energy, then think on these things. Perfection is not an outward quality, but an inward one.

I love God, therefore, everything I do must give Him glory and bring honor to His Name; never being out of order. Everything will exemplify the One I love; moving in sync with Him in order to bring the Kingdom into its fullness. Christian energy, must charge the atmosphere with positive energy so that whoever steps into my space will receive a super charge of the Holy Ghost. They will know they have been in the presence of the Lord.

Virtue takes work so that with the exercising of your faith, when someone comes into your presence, they will be healed and delivered. When in the press of the crowd, Jesus stated that somebody had touched Him. The disciples' response was that it was because Jesus was in such a large crowd. Virtue was removed from His body. The faith to believe is needed when things seem to be impossible. This does not require you to lay your hands on someone, but you should possess the wisdom to move as God directs you.

Virtue is a quality that develops you into spiritual maturity causing you to become a problem-solver, not the problem, by taking the Word of God and applying all of it to your life. Whatsoever things are pure, whatsoever things are just, and whatsoever things are honest; THINK on these things.

Every day, make yourself a promise: wherever you are today, do not be found in the same place tomorrow. Desire to grow. What trips you up will not do it again. Choose to be a better Christian today than you were yesterday.

7. Buy It, Buy It, Buy It

There are all kinds of schemes and self-improvement plans out there to help you feel better, to help you lose weight, to firm you up, and to help you to live longer. The advertisement industry shows how these products will do all this to improve your life, and they make it sound like this is just what you need. Testimonials of their products want you to believe that they will do so much for you and make you feel so much better.

I have discovered that people will spend, and try, anything to help themselves feel and look better. They will invest in a myriad of products, hoping to bring change to their present situation. The consumer industry has something for everything that ails you; some products even contain natural ingredients with nothing artificial in them. They challenge you to try their products for a certain number of days so that you will see how this product will improve this or that in you. After listening to how the product will make you feel better, then they have to disclose all of its side effects, which may even lead to death. Taking the product is supposed to help you live longer; but the side effects may cause the opposite result.

I found out that staying in the Word of God will heal you and have great side effects. Buy wisdom, and sell it not. It is life for you and will bring life more abundantly to you. The value of wisdom is more than gold and silver. The value of gold continues to increase in today's marketplace; it is not losing its value.

"If you seek [Wisdom] as for silver and search for skillful and godly Wisdom as for hidden treasures, Then you will understand the reverent and worshipful fear of the Lord and find the knowledge of [our omniscient] God." (Proverbs 2:4-5 AMP)

The bible has all the answers for everything that ails you. It amazes me how people will use the bible to disprove things; yet the Bible is what you need to live.

In Isaiah 55:1-3, the bible invites you come and drink if you are thirsty and have no money. Jesus releases a well, springing forth inside of you. Matthew 5:6 tells us that God's Word is a cure. Just pick it up, read it, and apply it in your life. Taking it every day brings a healthier environment and changes the atmosphere daily.

"For wisdom is a defense even as money is a defense, but the excellency of knowledge is that wisdom shields and preserves the life of him who has it." (Ecclesiastes 7:12 AMP)

"For by me [Wisdom from God] your days shall be multiplied, and the years of your life shall be increased." (Proverbs 9:11 AMP)

"Making the very most of the time [buying up each opportunity], because the days are evil." (Ephesians 5:16 AMP)

The world offers many quick fixes and supplements, but the Word of God offers great results.

"Buy the truth and sell it not; not only that, but also get discernment and judgment, instruction and understanding." (Proverbs 23:23 AMP)

In order to increase in all areas of life, wisdom needs to be applied. In today's fast-track society, we're told that you can obtain the real important nuggets for free; just pay the shipping and handling charges. The requirement for us is to be steadfast and unmovable towards obtaining all that God has for us. I beseech you, before going and buying these other products, invest your time in seeking the will of God for your life. This will bring you closer to your destiny. The Word of God will release your daily supply. Your order will always be filled, because Jesus died so that we will be complete and lack nothing.

The best advertisement is to see you up and giving God praise, for the ultimate price was paid. All God asks is for you to love Him with all your heart, soul, mind, body, and strength. Keep taking your 'gos-pills' to keep up with all that God is going to do with you.

8. Mother Wit

You may wonder, what in the world is 'Mother Wit.' In my terminology, mother wit is just plain old common sense; the ability to think things through before proceeding to do them; weighing a matter and then learning to choose my battles; and knowing how to fight to win them.

There are several instances in the scriptures that come to mind. The story of Hannah is a common sense episode. You have a man named Elkanah that has two women in His life. He is married to both; and one wife, Peninnah has children, but Hannah, the other wife, has none. Peninnah chooses to pick on Hannah because she is barren. Now, I should note that Elkanah actually loved Hannah more, and he tried to comfort her.

There are some things you must pursue if you want them. Hannah had to make a choice: either get back at Peninnah, or pursue the greater matter. I am thankful she chose to pursue the greater matter. She went to the temple to seek God concerning herself. Now, this is a selah moment. She did not go to a girlfriend, prayer partner, or some other associates. Now, it is okay to do that, if this is where you are, but Hannah went to a place where she was not supposed to be. While she was crying out to God, not uttering a word but pouring out her inner most being, Eli thought she was drunk. However, that was not the case. Desiring God more and wanting an answer from Him, Hannah made a promise to God that if He would give her a man child, she would give the child back to Him. The story goes on to say that Hannah went home to be with her husband, she then conceived and brought forth Samuel. After weaning him, she kept her promise and brought Samuel back to the temple. Furthermore, she also had more children.

What I received from this was the fact that Hannah went past the priest, and went straight to God. Now remember, the veil of the temple had not yet been rent. God is showing us that we can enter the Holy of Holies to make our requests known unto Him. Hannah birthed more than just a child. She set up a presidency.

When you cannot express to others what your heart is feeling, you have a God that hears and sees all. She chose not to bicker with Peninnah, but to go after God. WOW! If we could get women and men to see this today, we would have a life transformation revival going on. Stop letting other people set what is important to you, keeping you off focus and focus on things that are not important.

We do not own anyone, and you cannot stop people from doing what they want to do. So, mother wit would say, gather yourselves up and take care of what is best for you. God will work it out for you. The decision to take it to God is your responsibility.

"And Hannah prayed and said: 'My heart rejoices in the LORD; My horn is exalted in the LORD. I smile at my enemies, Because I rejoice in Your salvation. No one is holy like the LORD, For there is none besides You, Nor is there any rock like our God. Talk no more so very proudly; Let no arrogance come from your mouth, For the LORD is the God

of knowledge; And by Him actions are weighed. The bows of the mighty men are broken, And those who stumbled are girded with strength. Those who were full have hired themselves out for bread, And the hungry have ceased to hunger. Even the barren has borne seven, And she who has many children has become feeble. The LORD kills and makes alive; He brings down to the grave and brings up. The LORD makes poor and makes rich; He brings low and lifts up. He raises the poor from the dust And lifts the beggar from the ash heap, To set them among princes And make them inherit the throne of glory. For the pillars of the earth are the LORD's, And He has set the world upon them. He will guard the feet of His saints, But the wicked shall be silent in darkness. For by strength no man shall prevail. The adversaries of the LORD shall be broken in pieces; From heaven He will thunder against them. The LORD will judge the ends of the earth. He will give strength to His king, And exalt the horn of His anointed. Then Elkanah went to his house at Ramah. But the child ministered to the LORD before Eli the priest." (I Samuel 2:1-11)

The second story is taken from 2 Samuel 20:14-22.

"And he went through all the tribes of Israel to Abel and Beth Maachah and all the Berites. So they were gathered together and also went after Sheba. Then they came and besieged him in Abel of Beth Maachah; and they cast up a siege mound against the city, and it stood by the rampart. And all the people who were with Joab battered the wall to throw it down. Then a wise woman cried out from the city, "Hear, hear! Please say to Joab, 'Come nearby, that I may speak with you.'" When he had come near to her, the woman said, "Are you Joab?" He answered, "I am." Then she said to him, "Hear the words of your maidservant." And he answered, "I am listening." So she spoke, saying, "They used to talk in former times, saying, 'They shall surely seek guidance at Abel,' and so they would end disputes. I am

49

among the peaceable and faithful in Israel. You seek to destroy a city and a mother in Israel. Why would you swallow up the inheritance of the LORD?" And Joab answered and said, "Far be it, far be it from me, that I should swallow up or destroy! That is not so. But a man from the mountains of Ephraim, Sheba the son of Bichri by name, has raised his hand against the king, against David. Deliver him only, and I will depart from the city." So the woman said to Joab, "Watch, his head will be thrown to you over the wall." Then the woman in her wisdom went to all the people. And they cut off the head of Sheba the son of Bichri, and threw it out to Joab. Then he blew a trumpet, and they withdrew from the city, every man to his tent. So Joab returned to the king at Jerusalem." (2 Samuel 20:14-22)

This scripture talks about Joab and how they were going to battle Sheba's son. The city was besieged and they began to beat the wall down. (Joab did not play: you mess with the king, you are on his hit list.) The story goes on to say that a wise woman cried out from the city and asked for Joab to listen to what she had to say. She goes on to say that she is among the peaceable and faithful in Israel, and asked why Joab wanted to destroy the whole city for just one person. Joab responded by telling her to bring the man that came against the King to him. The woman's reply was that Joab watch, because his head would be thrown over the wall to him. The woman went to the people, who all got together and cut the man's head off and threw it over the wall.

The moral to this story is, "an ounce of prevention is worth a pound of cure." This means, she took on the task of finding out what Joab was after so that the city and her family would be spared, and that only the guilty would be punished and not the whole town.

Mother wit can also be used today to solve many issues. All that is required is to see what actions need to be in place in

50

order to spare someone's life or bring about a solution to a conflict. Good old common sense needs to find its place back in us.

CONCLUSION

It is critical to regain ground that has been lost in order to get back to the basics. We have to get closer to God. The only way to do that is to restore, refocus, and replenish wisdom in our churches and in our leaders.

"Come now, and let us reason together," Says the LORD, "Though your sins are like scarlet, they shall be as white as snow; though they are red like crimson, they shall be as wool." (Isaiah 1:18)

This scripture encourages us to come and reason together and to establish a dialogue about a situation before moving out or saying something we cannot retract. I believe that many hurts and disappointments can be avoided by simply thinking and not making flesh decisions.

More times than we can count, decisions are made without thinking about our responses, our reactions, or the consequences. This book shares with us about letting the wisdom of God speak to us, before we say one thing.

This Book causes us to allow wisdom to hold her place in our lives again.

BIBLIOGRAPHY

New American Standard Bible, Updated Edition, 1995.

Exhaustive Concordance of the Bible, Lahabra, CA: The Lockman Foundation--Foundation Publications, Inc., Anaheim, CA, 1981, 1998.

The Spirit Filled Bible (NKJV), Nelson Publishing, 2002.

The Amplified Bible, Zondervan and the Lockman Foundation, Grand Rapids, MI, 1987.

About the Author

Dr. Laura M. Thompson has been and is an unquestionable vessel of God. Affirmed by the Father, she is successfully running the course to which He has appointed her.

In 1984, Dr. Thompson surrendered to the mantle upon her life and acknowledged the call into the gospel ministry. Today she pastors one of most successful ministries in Sheffield, Alabama. Committed to produce the Spirit of Excellence Open Door Church is truly a house of refuge for the lost and broken. Dr. Thompson's first covenant with God is to usher a fresh wind of the Holy Spirit, flowing very fluently in the prophetic. Secondly, God has given her a Prophetic mandate to release proverbial truths like firmly embedded nails for the mastering of assemblies. The Father has also crowned her head with wisdom to make her a mother in Zion, because she possesses a travailing anointing to enable the church of the 21st century to rise to its fullest potential.

Dr. Laura M. Thompson is indeed a very powerful and anointed woman of God. Her number one goal is to gain one billion souls for the body of Christ and establish a place of refuge for His people. She also desires to establish and make ready the Church for the Lord's end-time harvest. As she continues to advance the Kingdom, she also wants to be a living pool of Bethesda so that whosoever steps into her presence shall be made whole. She is happily married to Mr. Marvin D. Thompson, she the mother of two adult daughters, and the proud grandmother of four grandsons and two granddaughters. She has a host of spiritual sons and daughters.

Dr. Laura M. Thompson is the author of *90 Days with Christ: Transforming Lives Through the Power and Love of Jesus Christ* and *Wisdom: It Is Not For Sale.*

For a complete listing of CDs, DVDs, and books by Dr. Laura Thomspon, or to particiapte in a ministry conference, book a conference, speaking event or training event, please send an email to:

apostlecore@yahoo.com

Books by Dr. Laura Thompson

90 Days With Christ
Wisdom: It Is Not For Sale

Laura Thompson Ministries ™